ECLIPSE

Towards the edge of the visible

Darren Almond

Miroslaw Balka

Raoul De Keyser

Isa Genzken

Felix Gonzalez-Torres

David Hammons

Mona Hatoum

Runa Islam

Sergej Jensen

Agnes Martin

Paul Pfeiffer

Andreas Slominski

Neal Tait

Cerith Wyn Evans

Darren Almond
Clock, 1997

Miroslaw Balka
"113 x 60 x 42", 2002

Miroslaw Balka
"60 x 50 x 35", 2003

Raoul De Keyser
Untitled, 1998

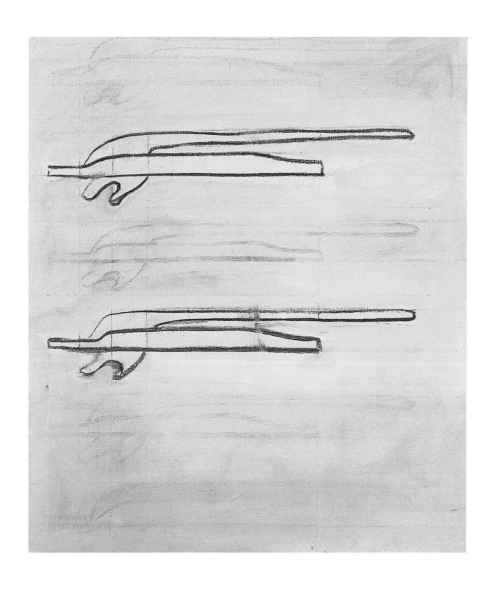

Raoul De Keyser
Closerie VIII (Berliner Ensemble), 1998

Isa Genzken
Sophienterrasse, 1991 & **Mittelweg**, 1991

Felix Gonzalez-Torres
"Untitled" (Perfect Lovers), 1987-1990

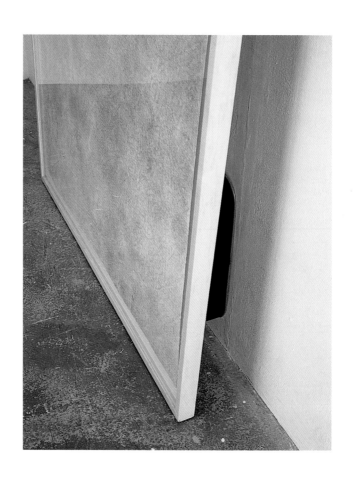

David Hammons
Traveling, 2002

David Hammons
Phat Free, 1995-1999

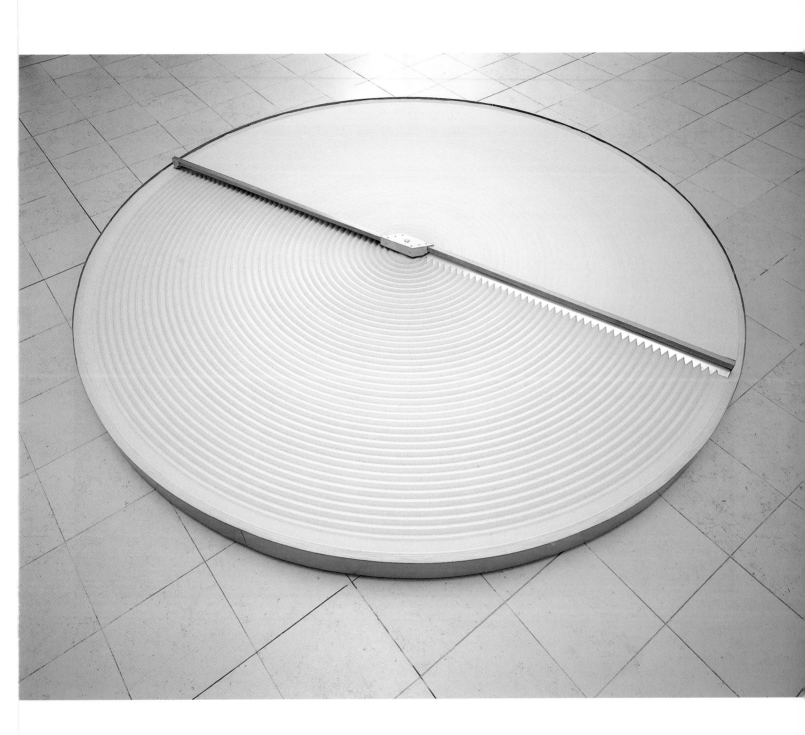

Mona Hatoum
+ **and** –, 1994-2004

24   Sergej Jensen
Untitled, 2002

Sergej Jensen
Schmoll, 2002

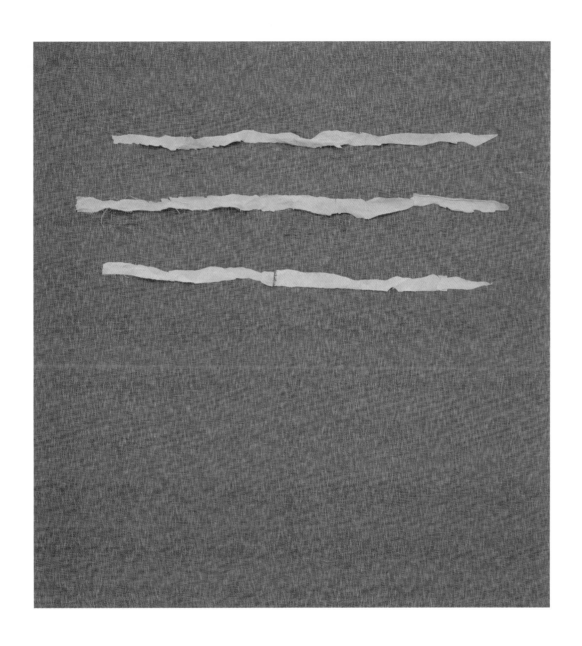

Sergej Jensen
The Last Kind Words, 2004

26   Agnes Martin
Untitled, 1978

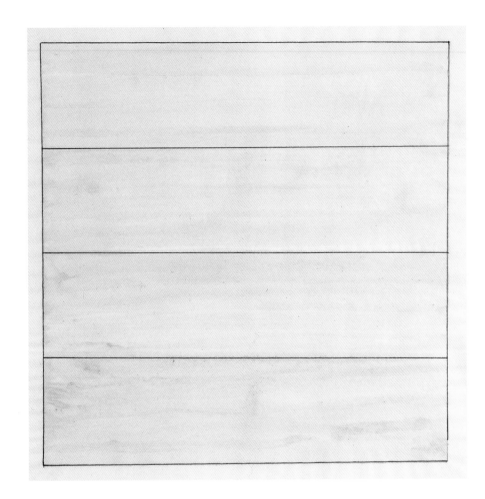

Agnes Martin
Untitled, 1995

Paul Pfeiffer
The Long Count III (Thrilla in Manila), 2001

Paul Pfeiffer
The Long Count (I Shook Up The World), 2000

Paul Pfeiffer
Four Horsemen of the Apocalypse, 2000

Andreas Slominski
Untitled, 1999

Andreas Slominski
Gestohlene Luftpumpe (Stolen Bicycle Pump), 1998

Neal Tait
Century 21, 2001

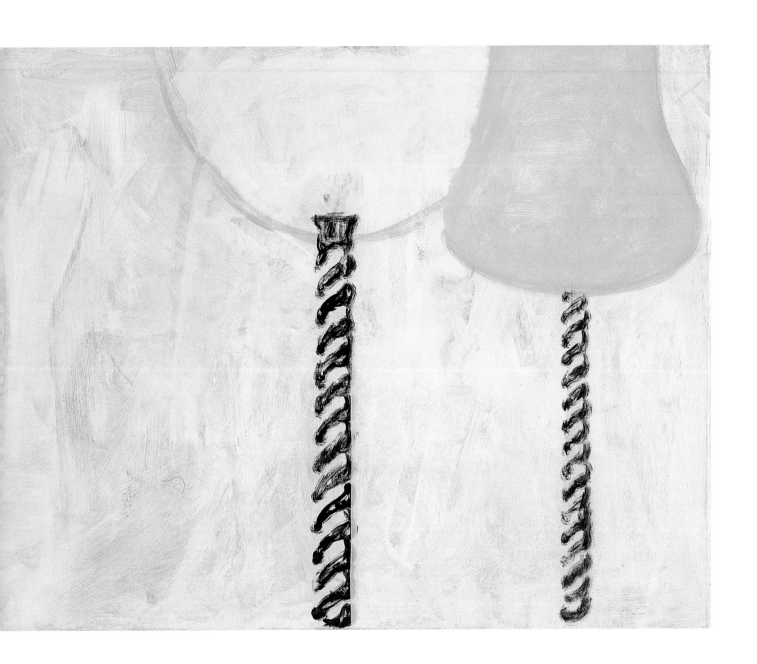

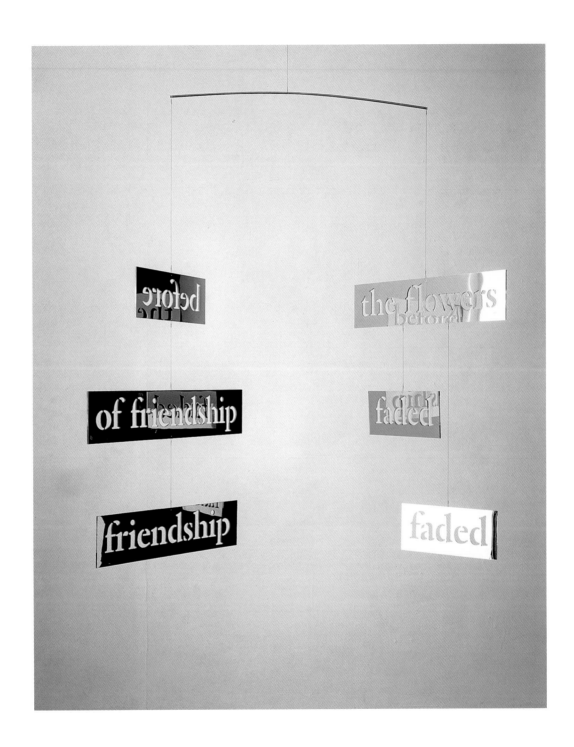

Cerith Wyn Evans
Before the Flowers of Friendship Faded, Friendship Faded, 2001

44   Cerith Wyn Evans
Miss Dawn Lewis, 2004

I call your image to mind

call and recall

Tactile and olfactory signs

I list your numerable

And innumerable parts...

I invoke

I summon your side effects

Summon and apply

Resonance and slapback

I summon illusions

Especially the flimsy underpinnings

of temporary things

I invoke I invoke I invoke

Cerith Wyn Evans
11.08.99, Munich (Total eclipse), 2004

ECLIPSE
Towards the edge of the visible

Annushka Shani

A lunar eclipse interrupts the everyday; the earth, moon and sun align so that as the moon crosses between the earth and sun, it casts them into shade. New conditions are momentarily set up and a reversal occurs as the sky takes on an eerie twilight, as if day were night. With the source of the visible veiled, other things come into view. In Cerith Wyn Evans' photograph of the shadows cast by trees taken during an eclipse, we see their patterns are composed of hundreds of eclipsed suns: the spaces between the leaves and branches of the trees were activated to perform as so many pinhole cameras.

'Eclipse' is a metaphor for a different kind of seeing and experiencing, something described in an account by the poet Elizabeth Bishop[1]:

'I watched closely the spaces between the birds. It was as if there were an invisible thread joining all the outside birds and within this fragile network they possessed the sky; it was down among them, of a paler colour, moving with them. The interspaces moved in pulsation too, catching up and continuing the motion of the wings in wakes, carrying it on, as the rest in music does – not blankness but a space as musical as all the sound.'

The fourteen artists in *Eclipse* belong to different generations and work in diverse media including painting, drawing, sculpture, film and performance, and yet they share an ear and eye for the subtle interpenetration things, the silent ground. They make works that cross borders into different realms, opening up the in-between spaces where shadows fall between visible and invisible, the image and its undoing, the mark and its erasure, the action and its trace. Because these works inhabit transitional spaces, they disrupt notions of static visual space and the absolute measure of the grid, instead revealing other less visual and more liminal, fluid and experiential structuring devices, such as boundary, trace, beat, cycle, frame, index, and horizon.

When absolute measures do appear – such as time or the grid – they are usually interrupted. In his work "*Untitled*" *(Perfect Lovers)* (1987-1990), Felix Gonzalez-Torres furtively subverts time's singular authority by placing side by side two identical clocks that are synchronised and tick away in harmony, mirroring each other's uninterrupted continuity. Like perfect lovers, the clocks seem to possess a mutual correspondence that nothing can disturb, yet as the exhibition continues, they imperceptibly move out of time and a gap opens between them. Time is again disturbed in Darren Almond's *Clock* (1997), a digital flip-clock that amplifies the mechanical sound of the turning hour, interrupting the silent flow of time so we can hear it passing. As severe and impassive as any minimalist object, the clock is also a poignant meditation on the relentless passage of time.

When the grid does appear, it is imperfect rather than ideal; we see it as irregular fluid channels of bleached colour stained onto the coarse material surface of Sergej Jensen's paintings, or implied in the whisper-quiet drawings of Agnes Martin, where almost imperceptible horizontal lines suggest infinite space beyond the serial grid. Through a simple geometry, Martin creates transparent and even fields of vision that somehow convey the intangible quality of subtle feelings: lucid and still.

Throughout the exhibition, we see the image undone. In Runa Islam's film projection *Stare Out (Blink)* (1998), the image is continually lost and found. An endless loop plays in which the blinding negative image of a young girl's face flashes momentarily onto the screen, then flashes off, leaving a blank white screen onto which we project the positive after-image. With this chiasma of vision, the viewer is transformed from the passive receiver of the image into its active transmitter; we also see that only through the negative can the positive appear. When the image does appear, it is with the sudden brevity of a vision: fugitive and provisional, it does not hold.

Cerith Wyn Evans' mirror mobile entitled *I call your image to mind, call and recall* (2004) also conjures the image. The words of the title are cut out of several rectangular mirrored bars that together hang in the gallery space, continually shifting, reflecting and refracting so that words move out of sequence, intersect, obscure each other and, on their edges, disappear. With its syntax interrupted and words emptied, we linger in the spaces of this broken evocation. It holds the image both in tantalising proximity and at a distance that never diminishes.

In Paul Pfeiffer's video work *The Long Count (I Shook Up the World)* (2000), the image undergoes an extreme erasure. The original television broadcast of one of Muhammad Ali's major championship fights has been digitally edited so that the bodies of both boxers are deleted as objects of spectacular fixation. With their substance leached away, an etherealised, spectral plasma pulses and tremors across the screen. Pfeiffer uses digital editing to address questions of historical visibility and invisibility, connecting themes of race, religion and art. The artist has said that he thinks of the spectacle as a kind of forgetting. By removing the bodies of both boxers he interrupts it, giving us back its negative hallucination.

In Pfeiffer's photographic work *Four Horseman of the Apocalypse* (2000), the image becomes even less tangible, appearing like an abstract landscape; it is, in fact, a reworked publicity shot of Marilyn Monroe on the beach, with her figure digitally erased. Pfeiffer describes the process as more akin to camouflaging than erasing, since through a painstaking procedure he overlays the figure with pieces of the background. Even though the artist drives the image underground – literally burying it – it seems to endure, latent, behind the scenes, yet active like some phantom limb.[2]

In Neal Tait's quiet, inward paintings the images lack fixity and appear to be recalled and reclaimed. Tait often finds his subjects in the overlooked and the unseen, things on the edges of vision that we perhaps cut out as visual noise: a pile of objects in the corner of a room, a broken TV aerial, a newspaper cutting – ordinary everyday things that are easily forgotten. Although these commonplace and dislocated things may provide the starting point for a picture, the actual images that surface in the paintings are discovered through the painting process, they feel recovered; as they emerge, these images sometimes mutate and conjoin with others, or become partially lost or erased. Tait's work engenders a haptic kind of vision, triggering fleeting, almost forgotten, memory sensations.

Similarly, Miroslaw Balka's sculptures are somehow able to give tangible form to feelings and memories that escape language. Often simple constructions, Balka's sculptures are made out of humble ready-to-hand materials, such as wooden sticks, stone slabs, a metal hoop and a drinking glass. He thinks of his sculptures as words in a sentence, so their placement and the spaces between them are crucial to their meaning. They often appear melancholic and work to transform the hard and specific space of the gallery into something more yielding, an associative place that acts as a container for histories as well as personal and collective memories. The

works carry a physical trace of the artist since he often finds their measures – titles, scale and placement – in the dimensions of his own body.

In contrast to the intimacy of Balka's work, Isa Genzken's twin architectonic sculptures, *Sophienterrasse* (1991) and *Mittelweg* (1991), convey a remarkable openness: two airy concrete constructions – at once fragile and severe. These hieratic, frame-like structures mark an interface between interior and exterior, articulating the play of structure and silhouette, materiality and space. With these two sculptures Genzken creates space without building it; they reveal how the transparent voids and interspaces are as vital constituents of the work as the material structure itself. Their frame-like constructions perform as both window and screen: windows that give a series of expansive 'filmic' views, and screens that set boundaries and divide space – including and excluding, separating and protecting. The two street names after which the sculptures are named fix a field of reference for the work as an urban environment – perhaps familiar to the artist – where public and private, social and aesthetic concerns meet.[3]

The artists in this exhibition all make works that open up in-between spaces and inhabit an interface or boundary, but they do so in very different ways and for different reasons; each artist communicates their own particular complex of space, idea and experience. In this sense it might be said that the show functions like a 'heterotopia', Foucault's concept of a contradictory site that is "capable of juxtaposing in a single real place several spaces, several sites that are in themselves incompatible". The theatre, cinema and garden are examples, as is the exhibition space when it both holds and juxtaposes works that carry disjunctive and discontinuous spaces and times.[4]

Mona Hatoum's kinetic sculpture *+ and -* (1994-2004) also marks an interface between the mark and its erasure. It is a circular, floor-based structure filled with sand across which a motor-driven arm slowly rotates; grooved on one end and flat on the other, as the arm turns it rakes circular lines into the bed of sand and simultaneously erases them, caught in a vicious cycle of drawing and erasure, recovery and denial. Hatoum's sculpture conveys a sense of the fragility and lightness of being; an abstract meditation on the unity of opposites such as yin and yang, *+ and -* is a perfectly-balanced closed system that possesses the meditative remove of a Buddhist wheel of life. It leaves a traceless trace.

Thinking about traces brings to mind theorist Rosalind Krauss's essay 'Notes on the Index', in which she defines the 'index' as the physical evidence or manifestation of something 'that has been', a prior cause that is no longer there. Imprints, traces, shadow and clues, as well as photographs and filmed performances, are examples of the indexical, and many of the works in this exhibition gather under this sign.[5] David Hammons' video work *Phat Free* (1995-1999) records a simple performance in which he kicks a metal bucket down an empty street at night, establishing a musical pattern like an improvised jazz solo. Hammons' drawing *Traveling* (2002) was made by throwing a basketball covered in graphite and dirt from the street at a tall sheet of paper. We can follow the invisible course of the ball and almost hear its beat travelling across the paper: hitting fast and slow, light and hard. These all-over marks gather densely in the drawing's higher half, lightening and breaking up below; the impression is of broken cloud on a grey day. These marks are at once indexical of what Louise Neri describes in a commentary on this piece as 'the artists presence, a sign of 'blackness', and piece of Harlem.'[6]

In a different way, Andreas Slominski's works are indexes of his ultra-light performative gestures. Slominski often presents objects and sculpture like enigmatic clues to some prior transgression, which might be simply a breaking with 'common-sense' rules, such as presenting a deceptively ordinary wall that has in fact been built from the top down. His *Gestohlene Luftpumpe (Stolen Bicycle Pump)* (1998) is a purloined and part-object, a relic which functions as an 'index' of the absent bike, a specific proof of the actual theft and evidence of the lunatic dimension to the artist's creative endeavour; on closer inspection we can see that instead of simply lifting the pump from its bracket, Slominski made the task more difficult for himself by sawing off the entire crossbar.

The elegant simplicity of Raoul De Keyser's paintings belies all the experiment and modifications involved in their making through the final pictorial sealing of the image in flat colour. We might sense this concealed history through the sedimented layers of the paint, but it is held like a secret. This history is revealed in *Closerie VIII (Berliner Ensemble)* (1998) (a charcoal and gesso picture that De Keyser insists is some-where between a drawing and a painting): two abstracted shapes resembling window fastenings fix the picture like a dual horizon, and around and beneath these images we see all the faint but still perceptible traces of where the same motif has been drawn, altered, over-painted and deleted. The work conveys an idea about space articulated eloquently by Henri Lefebvre when he said 'Nothing disappears completely (...) nor can what subsists be defined solely in terms of traces, memories or relics. In space, what came earlier continues to underpin what follows.'[7]

Together the artists in *Eclipse* make works that allow us to linger in the enabling gaps, pauses and silences between things. They inhabit unclear shadow lands where things are veiled and fall out of view.

'Every something is an echo of nothing.'[8] John Cage

1. Bishop's account was quoted by Felix Gonzalez-Torres in a fax he sent to a friend, a piece of correspondence mentioned by Lisa Corrin on page 8 of the catalogue to an exhibition of Gonzalez-Torres's work at the Serpentine Gallery, London in 2000.

2. See interview with Paul Pfeiffer published on the *Art:21* website at www.pbs.org/art21

3. See pp.74-79 of Christiane Schneider and Isa Genzken's catalogue to *KölnSkulptur 2* (Gesellschaft der Freunde des Skulpturenparks, Cologne, 1999).

4. See Michel Foucault, 'Of Other Spaces' (1967) (published in *Architecture/ Mouvement/Continuité*, October 1984; trans. Jay Miskowiec).

5. See p.211 of Rosalind E. Krauss, 'Notes on the Index: Part 2' in *The Originality of the Avant-Garde and Other Modernist Myths* (MIT Press, 1986).

6. See p.16 of Louise Neri, 'Concrete Poetry,' *Antipodes – Inside the White Cube* (Jay Jopling/White Cube, London 2003).

7. See pp.231-32 in Henri Lefebvre, *The Production of Space* (Blackwell, Oxford 1991; trans. Donald Nicholson-Smith).

8. See John Cage, *Silence: Lectures and Writings by John Cage* (Wesleyan University Press, 1961).

Darren Almond

Born in Wigan, England in 1971, Darren Almond graduated from Winchester School of Art in 1993. Since his first solo exhibition at White Cube, London in 1997 Almond has had solo exhibitions in both Europe and America including the Chisenhale Gallery, London (2000); Kunsthalle Zürich; De Appel Foundation, Amsterdam; Tate Britain, London (all 2001) and Fondazione Nicola Trussardi, Milan (2003). Almond lives and works in London.

Clock
1997
Perpsex, infra-red, sound stores and electric motor
31 x 41 x 20 cm

Miroslaw Balka

Miroslaw Balka was born in 1958 in Poland and trained at the Academy of Fine Arts in Warsaw. He has exhibited in numerous solo and group exhibitions internationally. Solo shows have included the National Museum of Art, Osaka, Japan (2000); Kröller-Müller Museum, Otterlo, The Netherlands and SMAK, Gent (both 2001); Douglas Hyde Gallery, Dublin; Museum of Contemporary Art, Zagreb and Dundee Contemporary Arts, Dundee (all 2002). Balka lives and works in Warsaw.

"60 x 50 x 35"
2003
Steel and glass
60 x 50 x 35 cm

"113 x 60 x 42"
2002
Terrazzo, wood and chewing gum
113 x 60 x 42 cm

Raoul De Keyser

Raoul De Keyser was born in 1930 in Belgium. He has exhibited in many international group shows such as *Documenta IX*, Kassel (1992); *Der Zerbrochene Spiegel. Positionen zur Malerei*, Kunsthalle Wien, Vienna and Deichtorhallen, Hamburg (1993) and *Unbound. Possibilities in Painting*, Hayward Gallery, London (1994). De Keyser has had numerous solo shows in Europe and America, the most recent being his solo show at the Whitechapel Gallery, London in 2004. He currently lives and works in Deinze, Belgium.

Closerie VIII (Berliner Ensemble)
1998
Gesso, charcoal, fixative on canvas
63 x 55 cm

Untitled
1998
Oil on canvas
55 x 50 cm

Isa Genzken

Isa Genzken was born in 1948 in Bad Oldesloe, Germany. She studied at the Berlin University of the Arts and the Düsseldorf State Art Academy. Solo exhibitions have been staged at the Palais des Beaux Arts, Brussels (1993); Frankfurter Kunstverein, Frankfurt (2000); Museum Ludwig, Cologne (2001) and Kunsthalle Zürich (2003). Genzken was also included in the *7th Istanbul Biennale* (2001); *Documenta XI*, Kassel (2002) and the *50th Venice Biennale* (2003) and will be included in the *Carnegie International*, Pittsburgh (2004). Isa Genzken lives and works in Berlin.

Sophienterrasse & **Mittelweg**
1991
Each part concrete and metal
Each in two parts: 262 x 56 x 8 cm

Felix Gonzalez-Torres

Felix Gonzalez-Torres (1957-1996) was born in Guaimaro, Cuba and educated in New York. His work has been exhibited internationally in numerous group and solo exhibitions. In 1994 a touring exhibition was organised by the Museum of Contemporary Art, Los Angeles which travelled to the Hirshhorn Museum and Sculpture Garden, Washington D.C. and the Renaissance Society at the University of Chicago. In 1995 a major retrospective exhibition was staged by the Solomon R. Guggenheim Museum in New York , which travelled to Centro Galego de Arte Contemporaneo, Santiago de Compostella (1995) and the Musée d'Art Moderne de la Ville de Paris (1996). In 2000 his work was shown at the Serpentine Gallery, London.

"Untitled" (Perfect Lovers)
1987-1990
Wall clocks
Two parts: 34.3 cm diameter each
Overall: 34.3 x 68.6 x 3.1 cm

David Hammons

Born in 1943 in Springfield, Illinois, David Hammons studied in Los Angeles and then at Parsons School of Design in New York. Major projects include Salzburger Kunstverein, Salzburg (1995); Kunsthalle Bern (1998) and the Museo Reina Sofia, Madrid (2000). His exhibition in Inside the White Cube in 2002 was his first solo show in London. Hammons lives and works in New York.

Traveling
2002
Harlem earth on paper and suitcase
295 x 124.5 x 21.5 cm

Phat Free
1995-1999
Single-channel DVD with sound
Duration: 5 minutes 20 seconds

Mona Hatoum

Mona Hatoum was born into a Palestinian family in Beirut in 1952 and moved to London in 1975, where she studied at the Byam Shaw School of Art and the Slade School of Art. Hatoum's work has been exhibited widely in Europe, the United States and Canada. In 1997 a touring exhibition was organised by the Museum of Contemporary Art, Chicago, which travelled to the New Museum of Contemporary Art, New York; the Museum of Modern Art, Oxford and the Scottish National Gallery of Modern Art, Edinburgh. Other solo exhibitions include Centre Georges Pompidou, Paris (1994); Castello di Rivoli, Turin (1999); Tate Britain, London; SITE Santa Fe, New Mexico (both 2000) and Mass MOCA, Massachusetts (2001). In 2004 a major survey of her work was shown at Hamburger Kunsthalle, Hamburg, which toured to Kunstmuseum Bonn and Magasin 3, Stockholm. Hatoum lives and works in London.

+ and -
1994-2004
Steel, aluminium, sand and electric motor
Height: 27 x diam. 400 cm

Runa Islam

Runa Islam was born in 1970 in Dhaka, Bangladesh. She studied at Middlesex University followed by a studio programme at the Rijksakademie in Amsterdam. Islam has exhibited in group exhibitions at the Whitechapel Art Gallery, London (1999/2001); Hayward Gallery, London (2000); Tate Modern, London; Frankfurter Kunstverein, Frankfurt and Witte de With, Rotterdam (all 2001). In 2000 Islam had her first solo exhibition in the UK and was awarded the prize for the best project in Guarene Arte 2000 at Fondazione Sandretto Re Rebaudengo par l'Arte, Italy. Other solo shows include White Cube, London (2001); Kunstverein Bregenz and MIT List Visual Arts Center, Cambridge, Massachusetts (both 2003). Islam lives and works in London.

Stare Out (Blink)
1998
16mm film
Duration: 3 minutes

53

Sergej Jensen

Sergej Jensen was born in Maglegaard, Denmark in 1973 and studied at the Hochschule für Bildende Künste, Frankfurt am Main. Exhibitions have included *Urgent Painting*, ARC, Paris (2002); Museum Morsbroich (2003); *São Paulo Biennale*, Brazil and the Kunstverein Hamburg (both 2004). He has had solo exhibitions at Galerie Neu, Berlin (2001 and 2004). Jensen lives and works in Berlin.

Agnes Martin

Agnes Martin was born in 1912 in Canada. She studied and taught art at the University of New Mexico, before receiving her MA from Columbia University, New York. Martin has had major solo exhibitions in both Europe and the United States including the Museum of Modern Art, New York (1973); the Hayward Gallery, London (1977); and the Museum of Fine Arts, Sante Fe (1979/1998). Touring exhibitions have been organised by both the Stedelijk Museum, Amsterdam (1991-92) and the Whitney Museum of American Art, New York (1992-94). Selected group exhibitions have included *American Drawings* at the Solomon R. Guggenheim, New York (1965-67) and *White on White* at the Museum of Contemporary Art, Chicago (1971). Martin represented USA at the *39th Venice Biennale* (1980) and has participated in both the *Whitney Biennale* and the *Carnegie International* on several occasions. Agnes Martin received the Golden Lion for Contribution to Contemporary Art at the 1997 *Venice Biennale* and the National Medal of Arts in 1998.

Paul Pfeiffer

Paul Pfeiffer was born in 1966 in Honolulu, Hawaii. In 1987 he studied at the San Francisco Art Institute and then in 1994 at Hunter College, New York, followed by the Whitney Independent Study Programme, New York. Group exhibitions have included the *Whitney Biennale*, New York (2000); *49th Venice Biennale* (2001) and *Cairo Biennale* (2003). Solo exhibitions and projects include Kunst-Werke, Berlin (2000); the Whitney Museum of American Art, New York; Kunsthaus Glarus (both 2001) and MIT List Visual Arts Center, Cambridge, Massachusetts (2003). Pfeiffer lives and works in New York.

Schmoll
2002
Chlorine on linen
140 x 110 cm

The Last Kind Words
2004
Linen
160 x 150 cm

Untitled
2002
Chlorine on jute
140 x 90 cm

Untitled
1978
Pencil on paper
28 x 28 cm

Untitled
1995
Pencil, ink and watercolour on paper
27.9 x 27.9 cm

Four Horsemen of the Apocalypse
2000
Cibachrome
149.9 x 119.4 cm

The Long Count (I Shook Up the World)
2000
LCD screen, videotape, mounting arm
15.2 x 17.8 x 152.4 cm
Duration approx: 5 minutes 57 seconds looped

The Long Count III (Thrilla in Manila)
2001
LCD screen, videotape, mounting arm
15.2 x 17.8 x 152.4 cm
Duration: 2 minutes 58 seconds looped

Andreas Slominski

Andreas Slominski was born in Meppen, Germany in 1959 and studied at the Hochschule für Bildende Künste in Hamburg. Solo shows have been held at the Hamburger Kunsthalle, Hamburg (1997); Kunsthalle Zürich (1998) and Deutsche Guggenheim, Berlin (1999). Slominski also made a project for the Münster Sculpture Park in 1997, the same year that he participated in the Venice Biennale. He lives and works in Hamburg.

Untitled
1999
Steel tube and glass of honey
160 x 35 cm diameter

Gestohlene Luftpumpe (Stolen Bicycle Pump)
1998
Metal, rubber and sticker
4 x 40 x 6 cm

Neal Tait

Neal Tait was born in Edinburgh in 1965 and studied at Chelsea School of Art and the Royal College of Art, London, where he graduated in 1993. Solo exhibitions have included White Cube, London in 2000 and 2003; Douglas Hyde Gallery, Dublin; Sies + Höke Galerie, Dusseldorf (both 2002) and Monica de Cardenas, Milan (2004). Recent group exhibitions include *Depiction*, Steirischer Herbst, Graz (2001); *Painting on the Move*, Kunsthalle Basel (2002) and *Atomkrieg*, Kunsthaus Dresden (2004). In 2001 he was awarded a residency at the British School at Rome. Tait lives and works in London.

Century
2001
Acrylic on canvas
60 x 70 cm

Girly Plots
2004
Acrylic and tempera on canvas
71.1 x 91.4 cm

Cerith Wyn Evans

Born in Wales in 1958, Cerith Wyn Evans graduated from the Royal College of Art, London in 1984. Wyn Evans has exhibited extensively in Europe and America including solo shows at Tate Britain, London (2000); Kunsthaus Glarus (2001); Camden Arts Centre, London and Frankfurter Kunstverein, Frankfurt, (both 2004). In 2002 he participated in *Documenta XI*, Kassel and in 2003 in the *50th Venice Biennale*. Wyn Evans lives and works in London.

Before the Flowers of Friendship Faded, Friendship Faded
2001
Mirror-coated perspex, wire and stainless steel rod
Dimensions variable

Miss Dawn Lewis
2004
Black and white photograph by Sulwyn Evans and text
Dimensions variable
(Paper size of photograph: 50.5 x 37.8 cm)

11.08.99, Munich (Total eclipse)
2004
C-print
49.6 x 33.3 cm

WHITE CUBE

48 Hoxton Square London N1 6PB

Tel +44 (0)20 7930 5373 Fax +44 (0)20 7749 7480

www.whitecube.com

Published by Jay Jopling/White Cube (London) to accompany the exhibition:

ECLIPSE
Towards the edge of the visible

16 July – 21 August 2004

Jay Jopling would like to extend special thanks to the artists; to all the staff at White Cube and in particular Annushka Shani. Thanks also to all the galleries who have assisted and cooperated with the preparation of this exhibition:

Artemis Greenberg Van Doren Gallery, New York
Galerie Daniel Buchholz, Cologne
Dallas Museum of Art, Dallas
Barbara Gladstone Gallery, New York
The Felix Gonzalez-Torres Foundation, New York
Galerie Neu, Berlin
PaceWildenstein, New York
The Project, New York
The Rachofsky Collection, Dallas
Galerie Zeno X, Antwerp

Other individuals who have helped in different ways: thanks to Miciah Hussey, Daniel Buchholz, Kate Carey, Frank Demaegd, Sima Familant, Katharina Forero, Jeanne Greenberg Rohatyn, Arne Glimcher, Barbara Gladstone, Carmen Hammons, Christian Haye, Ally Ireson, Jack Lane, Michelle Reyes, Howard & Cindy Rachofsky, Alexander Schroeder, Beth Taylor, Jeffrey Uslip, Thilo Wermke, Charles Wylie.

Reproductions of works supplied courtesy of Artemis Greenberg Van Doren Gallery, New York; Barbara Gladstone Gallery, New York; Galerie Barbara Weiss, Berlin; Deutsche Guggenheim, Berlin; Douglas Hyde Gallery, Dublin; The Felix Gonzalez-Torres Foundation, courtesy of Andrea Rosen Gallery, New York; Galerie Neu, Berlin; PaceWildenstein, New York; The Project, New York and Los Angeles.

Photography: Eberle & Einsfeld, Sarah Harper Gifford, Christoph Irrgang, John Kellett, Peter Muscato, Ellen Page Wilson, Stephen White, Jens Ziehe.

Cover image:
Cerith Wyn Evans, 11.08.99, Munich (Total eclipse), 2004

Exhibition selected and curated by Annushka Shani

Design: Miles Murray Sorrell FUEL

ISBN 0-9546501-3-1

Legends